I0480000

The Wealth Accelerator: Master Your Money and Catapult Your Success

Alice and SaPH

ISBN-13: 979-8-3870-0579-4

CONTENTS

1	Introduction	2
2	Chapter 1: The Mindset of the Wealthy	4
3	Common myths about money and wealth	6
4	How to develop a millionaire mindset	10
5	Strategies for overcoming limiting beliefs and negative thought patterns	14
6	Chapter 2: Mastering Your Money	16
7	Creating a budget and tracking your expenses	17
8	Strategies for saving money and building wealth over time	20
9	Tips for reducing debt and managing credit wisely	25
10	How to optimize your spending and increase your savings rate	27
11	Chapter 3: Building Your Financial Foundation	30
12	Setting financial goals and creating a plan to achieve them	32
13	Understanding the basics of investing and asset allocation	34
14	How to build a diversified investment portfolio	35
15	Chapter 4: Accelerating Your Financial Progress	37
16	Strategies for increasing your income and earning potential	38
17	Tips for creating multiple streams of income	43
18	How to leverage your skills and expertise to increase your earnings	45
19	The power of passive income and how to create it	46
20	Chapter 5: Staying Motivated and on Track	48
21	How to overcome obstacles and stay focused on your goals	51
22	Tools and resources for tracking your progress and staying accountable	53
23	Strategies for celebrating your successes and staying motivated for the long term	54
24	Conclusion	55
25	Recap of key takeaways from the book	56
26	Final words of advice for achieving financial success	57
27	How to continue learning and growing on your	58

financial journey.

Introduction

Welcome to The Wealth Accelerator, a comprehensive guide to mastering your money and catapulting your success. If you're looking to achieve financial freedom and build lasting wealth, then you're in the right place.

Why is building wealth important? Well, financial security can give you the freedom to pursue your passions, spend time with loved ones, and create the life you've always wanted. It can help you weather life's unexpected challenges, and provide a sense of stability and peace of mind.

But building wealth isn't always easy, and that's where this book comes in. In the following pages, you'll discover practical strategies, insights, and tips for mastering your money and accelerating your financial progress.

What can you expect from this book? You'll learn how to develop a millionaire mindset, master your money, build a solid financial foundation, and accelerate your progress towards your goals. You'll discover tips for increasing your income, creating multiple streams of income, and optimizing your spending to maximize your savings and investment potential.

How can you use this book to achieve your goals? Take the time to read each chapter thoroughly, and complete any exercises or activities that resonate with you. Consider sharing your progress with a trusted friend or family member for added accountability and support. And most importantly, don't be afraid to take action and make changes to your financial habits and behaviors based on what you learn here.

So let's get started on your journey to financial success. Whether you're just starting out on your financial journey or looking to take your wealth-building to the next level, "The Wealth Accelerator" is here to help you achieve your goals.

Chapter 1: The Mindset of the Wealthy

As the saying goes, "Your thoughts become your reality." This is especially true when it comes to building wealth. The mindset you have around money and wealth can make all the difference in achieving financial success.

In this chapter, we'll explore the importance of mindset in wealth-building, and why having the right mindset is essential for creating lasting wealth.

First, we'll discuss some common myths about money and wealth, and why these limiting beliefs can hold you back from achieving your goals. We'll then dive into strategies for developing a millionaire mindset, including techniques for overcoming negative thought patterns and limiting beliefs.

We'll also explore how mindset can impact your financial decisions, and how to make sure you're making choices that align with your financial goals. By the end of this chapter, you'll have a deeper understanding of the importance of mindset in wealth-building, and the tools you need to cultivate a mindset of abundance and success.

Common myths about money and wealth

We all have preconceived notions about money and wealth, many of which are not true. These myths can hold us back from making sound financial decisions and building lasting wealth. Here are some of the most common myths about money and wealth:

✦ Myth 1: Wealth is only for the lucky or the born rich

This is a common myth that can hold people back from pursuing their financial goals. The truth is that anyone can build wealth with the right mindset, strategies, and discipline. While some people may have a head start due to family wealth or other advantages, that doesn't mean you can't achieve financial success on your own.

In fact, many millionaires and billionaires started with little to no wealth and built their fortunes through hard work, determination, and smart financial decisions. They didn't rely on luck or inheritance to achieve success.

It's also worth noting that wealth isn't just about money. Wealth can mean different things to different people, such as having financial freedom, being able to travel and enjoy life, or being able to give back to others. Whatever your definition of wealth may be, know that it's within your reach if you're willing to put in the effort.

Don't let the myth that wealth is only for the lucky or the born rich hold you back. With the right mindset and strategies, you can achieve financial success and create a life of abundance and fulfillment. In the next section, we'll explore more myths about money and wealth and offer the truth behind them.

✦ Myth 2: You need a lot of money to start building wealth

This is another common myth that can hold people back from pursuing their financial goals. The truth is that building wealth is more about creating good habits than having a lot of money. Even small amounts of money can add up over time, so it's important to start saving and investing as early as possible.

In fact, the earlier you start saving and investing, the more time your money has to grow through compound interest. Compound interest is when you earn interest on both your initial investment and the interest that investment earns over time. This can lead to significant growth in your wealth over the long-term, even if you start with just a small amount of money.

It's also worth noting that building wealth isn't just about saving and investing. It's also about making smart financial decisions, such as living below your means, avoiding debt, and investing in assets that appreciate in value.

Don't let the myth that you need a lot of money to start building wealth hold you back. Start building good financial habits now, no matter how small your contributions may be, and you'll be on your way to creating a life of abundance and financial freedom. In the next section, we'll explore how to develop a millionaire mindset that supports your wealth-building goals.

✦ Myth 3: Debt is always bad

This is a myth that can be harmful to your financial health if taken at face value. While some types of debt, like high-interest credit card debt, can be detrimental to your financial wellbeing, not all debt is bad. In fact, taking on debt to invest in assets that appreciate in value, like a home or a business, can be a smart financial move.

The key is to differentiate between "good" debt and "bad" debt. Good debt is debt that helps you achieve your financial goals and has a positive impact on your net worth over time. For example, taking out a mortgage to buy a home can be considered good debt because it allows you to build equity in a valuable asset that is likely to appreciate in value over time.

Bad debt, on the other hand, is debt that has high-interest rates and does not contribute to your financial wellbeing. Examples of bad debt include credit card debt, payday loans, and car loans with high-interest rates.

It's important to be mindful of the debt you take on and to use debt strategically to achieve your financial goals. This means avoiding high-interest debt and taking on debt only when it is necessary and will contribute positively to your financial future.

Don't let the myth that debt is always bad hold you back. By understanding the difference between good debt and bad debt and using debt strategically, you can achieve your financial goals and build lasting wealth. In the next section, we'll explore how to develop the millionaire mindset that supports your financial success.

✦ Myth 4: Investing is too risky

Investing can seem intimidating, especially for those who are just starting to build their wealth. However, the truth is that investing is one of the best ways to build wealth over time. While it is true that investing involves some risk, there are ways to manage that risk and maximize your potential returns.

One of the keys to successful investing is diversification. By spreading your investments across different asset classes, industries, and geographies, you can reduce your overall risk and increase your potential for long-term gains. This means investing not only in stocks but also in bonds, real estate, and other asset classes.

Another key to successful investing is discipline. This means staying committed to your investment strategy and avoiding emotional decisions based on short-term market fluctuations. It also means staying patient and focused on your long-term goals, even in the face of temporary setbacks or downturns.

Investing does involve some risk, but the rewards can be substantial for those who approach it with a long-term perspective and a disciplined approach. By diversifying your investments and staying focused on your goals, you can manage risk and maximize your potential returns over time.

Now that we have debunked some of the common myths about wealth-building and explored the importance of mindset, let's dive into specific strategies for accelerating your wealth and achieving financial success.

By recognizing and dispelling these common myths, you can start to develop a more accurate and effective mindset when it comes to money and wealth-building. In the following sections, we'll explore strategies for cultivating a millionaire mindset and making sound financial decisions that align with your goals.

How to develop a millionaire mindset

Building wealth starts with your mindset. If you think like a millionaire, you're more likely to act like one and achieve financial success. Here are some strategies for developing a millionaire mindset:

✦ Think Big

If you want to build wealth and achieve financial success, it's important to think big. Millionaires don't settle for mediocrity, and neither should you. Instead, aim high and set ambitious goals that challenge you to grow and achieve more than you ever thought possible.

One of the first steps in thinking big is to develop a clear vision of what you want to achieve. This means defining your financial goals in detail and visualizing what your life will look like once you've achieved them. This vision will serve as a guiding light as you work towards your goals and will help keep you motivated and focused.

Another key to thinking big is to cultivate a mindset of abundance rather than scarcity. This means focusing on the opportunities that exist rather than the limitations. Instead of thinking about what you don't have or can't do, focus on what you do have and what you can do to achieve your goals.

It's also important to be willing to take risks and step outside your comfort zone. Building wealth requires taking action, and sometimes that means taking calculated risks and pursuing opportunities that may feel uncomfortable or unfamiliar. Don't let fear hold you back from achieving your goals.

Finally, surround yourself with people who think big and share your vision for success. Seek out mentors and role models who have achieved the kind of success you aspire to and learn from their experiences. And surround yourself with supportive friends and family members who encourage and motivate you to pursue your dreams.

Thinking big is essential for building wealth and achieving financial success. By developing a clear vision, cultivating a mindset of abundance, taking risks, and surrounding yourself with like-minded individuals, you can unlock your full potential and achieve more than you ever thought possible.

✦ Focus on Abundance

One of the keys to building wealth is to cultivate an abundance mindset. This means shifting your focus from what you lack to what you have and believing that there's enough to go around. By focusing on abundance, you can unlock your full potential and create the wealth and success you desire.

One of the first steps in cultivating an abundance mindset is to practice gratitude. Take time each day to appreciate the resources and opportunities you have in your life. Instead of dwelling on what you lack, focus on what you have and how you can use it to achieve your goals.

Another important aspect of an abundance mindset is to believe that there's enough to go around. This means letting go of the scarcity mentality that says there's only so much wealth and success to be had. Instead, focus on the abundance of opportunities and possibilities that exist and believe that you can create as much wealth as you need.

It's also important to be open to new ideas and opportunities. An abundance mindset is characterized by a sense of curiosity and a willingness to explore new paths and take risks. Don't be afraid to try new things and step outside your comfort zone in pursuit of your goals.

Finally, surround yourself with people who embody an abundance mindset. Seek out individuals who are optimistic, supportive, and believe in the power of abundance. These people can provide encouragement and motivation as you work towards your goals and help you stay focused on the possibilities rather than the limitations.

By focusing on abundance, cultivating gratitude, and embracing new opportunities, you can unlock your full potential and create the wealth and success you desire. With an abundance mindset, the possibilities are limitless.

✦ Taking Calculated Risks

Building wealth often requires taking risks, but not reckless ones. It's important to learn how to identify and assess risks and take calculated risks that have the potential for high rewards.

The first step in taking calculated risks is to do your research. Gather as much information as possible about the potential risks and rewards of an opportunity. Consult experts, analyze data, and consider different scenarios to evaluate the likelihood of success.

Once you've assessed the risks, it's important to weigh them against the potential rewards. Determine whether the potential payoff is worth the potential risks. Consider your financial situation, your goals, and your risk tolerance when making your decision.

Another key to taking calculated risks is to have a backup plan. Prepare for the worst-case scenario and have a contingency plan in place to minimize the potential damage if things don't go as planned. This can help reduce your overall risk and give you more confidence to take the leap.

It's also important to learn from your mistakes. Not every risk will pay off, but you can use the experience to improve your decision-making process in the future. Analyze what went wrong and identify what you could have done differently. This will help you make better decisions and take smarter risks in the future.

Finally, don't let fear hold you back. Fear of failure or the unknown can be paralyzing, but it's important to overcome these fears if you want to achieve success. Take calculated risks, trust your instincts, and have the confidence to pursue your goals with determination.

By taking calculated risks, you can open up new opportunities for wealth-building and achieve greater success in your financial endeavors. With the right mindset and approach, calculated risks can be a powerful tool for catapulting your wealth and success to new heights.

↓ Learn from failure

Learning from failure is a key part of developing a resilient and successful mindset when it comes to building wealth. By reframing failure as a learning opportunity and using setbacks as stepping stones to success, you can develop the resilience and adaptability you need to overcome obstacles and achieve your goals.

↓ Surround yourself with like-minded people

Surrounding yourself with like-minded people can be a great way to stay motivated and on track when it comes to building wealth. By seeking out mentors and role models who have achieved the kind of success you want, you can learn from their experiences and gain valuable insights into what it takes to succeed. Additionally, being part of a supportive community of like-minded individuals can help you stay focused on your goals and provide the encouragement and accountability you need to stay on track.

By implementing these strategies, you can start to develop a millionaire mindset and begin building lasting wealth. In the next section, we'll explore how mindset impacts your financial decisions and offer tips for making sound financial choices.

Strategies for overcoming limiting beliefs and negative thought patterns

Limiting beliefs and negative thought patterns can hold you back from achieving financial success. Here are some strategies for overcoming them:

Identifying limiting beliefs is a crucial first step in overcoming them and achieving success. By recognizing the beliefs and attitudes that are holding you back, you can begin to challenge them and develop a more positive and empowering mindset. Some common limiting beliefs around money and wealth include beliefs about scarcity, self-worth, and the morality of wealth. Once you've identified these beliefs, you can begin to examine them critically and replace them with more empowering beliefs that support your goals and aspirations.

Challenge your beliefs. Once you've identified your limiting beliefs, challenge them. Ask yourself if they're really true, and look for evidence to the contrary. For example, if you believe that money is evil, ask yourself if that's really the case, or if money can actually be used for good.

Additionally, you can seek out examples of people who have achieved financial success while still maintaining their values and making a positive impact in the world. This can help shift your perspective and challenge your limiting beliefs.

Reframe negative thoughts. Negative thoughts can quickly spiral out of control and lead to self-doubt and fear. Reframe negative thoughts into more positive, empowering ones. For example, instead of thinking "I'll never be able to afford that," reframe it as "What steps can I take to make that a reality?"

Practice positive affirmations

Positive affirmations can help to shift your mindset and reprogram your subconscious beliefs. Here are a few more examples of positive affirmations:

- o I am worthy of financial abundance and success.
- o I have everything I need to create the life I desire.
- o I am grateful for the wealth and abundance in my life.
- o I trust in my ability to make wise financial decisions.
- o I attract opportunities for financial growth and success.

Visualize success. Visualization is another effective technique for overcoming limiting beliefs and negative thought patterns. Visualize yourself achieving your financial goals in vivid detail, and feel the emotions of success as if they're already a reality.

By implementing these strategies, you can overcome limiting beliefs and negative thought patterns and start to develop a more positive, empowered mindset that supports your wealth-building goals. In the next section, we'll explore how to make sound financial decisions that align with your goals and values.

Chapter 2: Mastering Your Money

Creating a budget and tracking your expenses

Creating a budget and tracking your expenses are essential steps in mastering your money. A budget is a plan for your income and expenses, and tracking your expenses means keeping a record of where your money is going. Here are some tips for creating a budget and tracking your expenses:

✦ Determine your income

To determine your income, you should add up all of the money you earn in a month. This might include your salary or wages from your job, as well as any bonuses or commissions you receive. You should also include any other sources of income, such as rental income or money earned from a side hustle. Once you have a total for your monthly income, you can move on to the next step of creating a budget.

✦ List your expenses:

Make a list of all your monthly expenses, including fixed expenses like rent or mortgage payments, car payments, and insurance, as well as variable expenses like groceries, entertainment, and clothing.

✦ Categorize your expenses

Divide your expenses into categories, such as housing, transportation, food, entertainment, and savings.

Categorizing your expenses can help you see where your money is going and identify areas where you might be able to cut back. Some other common expense categories include utilities, healthcare, personal care, and debt payments. It's important to make sure you're accounting for all of your expenses, including irregular expenses like car repairs or medical bills.

⊥ Set spending limits

Based on your income and expenses, set spending limits for each category. This will help you prioritize your spending and avoid overspending.

Setting spending limits can be very helpful in managing your finances. It's important to ensure that your spending limits align with your financial goals and priorities. For example, if your priority is to save for a down payment on a house, you may need to set a lower spending limit for entertainment or eating out. Conversely, if your priority is to enjoy experiences with friends and family, you may allocate more of your budget towards entertainment. The key is to find a balance that works for you and helps you reach your financial goals.

⊥ Track your expenses

Keep track of all your expenses by saving receipts, using a budgeting app, or tracking expenses in a spreadsheet. This will help you stay on top of your spending and identify areas where you can cut back.

Tracking your expenses is crucial to staying within your budget and identifying areas where you may be overspending. It's important to record all of your expenses, no matter how small, so that you have an accurate picture of where your money is going. This will allow you to make informed decisions about where to cut back or reallocate funds.

⊥ Adjust your budget as needed

Your budget should be flexible and adaptable to changes in your income or expenses. Review your budget regularly and make adjustments as needed.

It's important to regularly review your budget and adjust it as needed to make sure you're staying on track and meeting your financial goals. Life circumstances can change, and your budget should be able to adapt to those changes. For example, if you get a raise, you may want to adjust your budget to increase your savings or pay down debt faster. Or if you have unexpected expenses, you may need to cut back on other areas of spending to make up for it.

By creating a budget and tracking your expenses, you'll have a better understanding of your financial situation and be better equipped to make informed decisions about your money.

Strategies for saving money and building wealth over time

⊥ Start with a savings plan

Set a specific savings goal and work towards it. Automate your savings by setting up automatic transfers from your checking account into a savings account or investment account.

starting with a savings plan is a great way to build wealth over time. Here are some additional strategies to consider:

- o **Start small:** Begin by saving a small amount each month and gradually increase it over time as you become more comfortable with your budget.

- o **Create an emergency fund:** Set aside 3-6 months' worth of living expenses in an emergency fund to protect yourself against unexpected expenses or job loss.

- o **Take advantage of employer benefits:** Contribute to your employer's 401(k) plan, especially if they offer a matching contribution.

- o **Invest in low-cost index funds:** Invest in low-cost index funds or exchange-traded funds (ETFs) to diversify your portfolio and minimize investment fees.

- o **Consider real estate investments:** Real estate can be a good long-term investment, especially if you're able to purchase a property that generates rental income.

- o **Reduce debt:** Pay down high-interest debt like credit card balances as quickly as possible, as the interest charges can eat away at your wealth-building efforts.

- o **Stay focused on your goals:** Keep your savings goals top of mind and avoid the temptation to overspend or take on unnecessary debt.

⚞ Cut back on expenses

Look for ways to reduce your expenses, such as cutting back on eating out or entertainment, negotiating bills or shopping around for better deals on services like insurance and utilities.

cutting back on expenses can help you save more money and build wealth over time. Here are some ways to cut back on expenses:

- o **Reduce your food expenses:** Consider eating out less often and cooking more meals at home. Plan your meals ahead of time and make a grocery list to avoid impulse purchases. You can also save money by buying in bulk or purchasing generic brands.

- o **Cut back on subscriptions:** Cancel subscriptions that you don't use or need, such as streaming services or magazine subscriptions.

- o **Reduce your transportation costs:** Consider carpooling, biking, or taking public transportation to reduce your transportation costs. You can also save money on gas by driving more efficiently and keeping your tires properly inflated.

- o **Negotiate bills:** Contact your service providers, such as your cable or internet provider, and negotiate a lower rate. You can also shop around for better deals on services like insurance and utilities.

- o **Use coupons and discount codes:** Look for coupons and discount codes before making purchases online or in-store. You can also sign up for loyalty programs to receive exclusive discounts and rewards.

⚞ Use credit wisely:

Avoid high-interest credit cards and use credit responsibly. Pay your bills on time and in full each month to avoid unnecessary interest charges.

Using credit responsibly is an essential strategy for saving money and building wealth over time. Here are some additional tips for using credit wisely:

- **Keep your credit utilization low:** Try to keep your credit card balances below 30% of your credit limit. This can help you maintain a good credit score and avoid high-interest charges.

- **Consider a balance transfer:** If you have high-interest credit card debt, consider transferring your balance to a card with a lower interest rate. This can help you save money on interest charges and pay off your debt more quickly.

- **Avoid unnecessary fees:** Read the fine print on your credit card agreement to avoid unnecessary fees, such as annual fees or balance transfer fees.

- **Use rewards wisely:** If you have a rewards credit card, use it strategically to earn cashback, points, or miles. But be sure to pay your balance in full each month to avoid interest charges that can offset any rewards you earn.

Invest in retirement accounts

Take advantage of retirement accounts like 401(k)s or IRAs to save for retirement. Contribute as much as you can afford to these accounts to take advantage of the tax benefits and compound interest over time.

Invest in other types of accounts

In addition to retirement accounts, consider investing in other types of accounts, such as brokerage accounts or real estate. Diversifying your investments can help reduce risk and maximize returns over the long term.

⊹ Set financial goals

Set specific financial goals for the short and long term, such as paying off debt, saving for a down payment on a house, or retiring comfortably. Having clear goals can help you stay motivated and focused on your financial plan.

⊹ Track your net worth

Calculate your net worth regularly by subtracting your liabilities from your assets. Tracking your net worth over time can help you monitor your progress and make adjustments to your financial plan as needed.

⊹ Stay informed

Keep up-to-date on financial news and trends, and seek advice from reputable sources. This can help you make informed decisions about your investments and financial plan.

⊹ Work with a financial advisor

Consider working with a financial advisor to help you develop a personalized financial plan, manage your investments, and stay on track towards your goals.

⊹ Diversify your investments

Don't put all your money into one type of investment or one company. Spread your investments across different types of assets and sectors to reduce risk and increase potential returns.

Diversifying your investments is an important strategy for building wealth over time. This means investing in a mix of stocks, bonds, real estate, and other assets to spread out risk and increase the potential for long-term gains. By diversifying, you can also protect your portfolio from the ups and downs of any one particular asset or sector. It's important to regularly review and rebalance your portfolio to ensure that your investments are still aligned with your goals and risk tolerance.

✦ Consider real estate

Additionally, investing in real estate can provide various tax benefits, such as mortgage interest deductions and depreciation write-offs. However, it's essential to do thorough research and due diligence before investing in real estate, as it can also come with risks and expenses. It's recommended to seek the advice of a real estate professional or financial advisor before making any significant investments in real estate.

✦ Stay focused on your goals

Building wealth takes time and patience. Stay focused on your goals and keep working towards them, even if progress seems slow at times. Remember that every little bit counts and small steps can add up to big gains over time.

Tips for reducing debt and managing credit wisely

Here are some tips for reducing debt and managing credit wisely:

✦ Create a budget

Having a budget is a crucial step in managing debt and improving your financial situation. By tracking your income and expenses, you can identify areas where you may be overspending and redirect those funds towards paying down debt. Additionally, setting aside money for savings can help you avoid going further into debt in case of unexpected expenses.

✦ Pay off high-interest debt first

Paying off high-interest debt first is an effective strategy because it helps you save money in interest charges over time. By eliminating high-interest debt, you can free up more money to pay off other debts and increase your overall financial flexibility. It's important to continue making minimum payments on all your debts while focusing on paying off the highest interest debt.

✦ Make more than the minimum payment

Always aim to pay more than the minimum payment on your credit cards and loans. This will help you pay off your debts faster and save money on interest charges.

✦ Negotiate lower interest rates

Contact your credit card companies or lenders and ask if they can lower your interest rate. This can help you save money on interest charges and pay off your debts faster.

Additionally, it may be helpful to research and compare credit cards or loans with lower interest rates and consider transferring your debt to a lower interest rate option if it makes sense for your financial situation. Keep in mind that some balance transfer options may come with fees or introductory rates that increase after a certain period, so be sure to read the fine print before making a decision.

✦ Consolidate your debt

Consider consolidating your debts into a single loan with a lower interest rate. This can help you simplify your payments and save money on interest charges.

✦ Use credit responsibly

Only use credit when you need to and pay your bills on time and in full each month to avoid unnecessary interest charges and fees.

✦ Monitor your credit score

Keep an eye on your credit score and report to identify any errors or fraud. A good credit score can help you qualify for lower interest rates and better loan terms.

How to optimize your spending and increase your savings rate

Optimizing your spending and increasing your savings rate involves finding ways to reduce your expenses and increase your income. Here are some tips:

- ↓ **Cut unnecessary expenses**: Look for ways to trim your budget, such as eating out less, cutting subscription services, and reducing utility costs.

  Here are some more ways to cut unnecessary expenses and optimize your spending:

  o **Create a shopping list:** Before you go grocery shopping or run errands, make a list of what you need to buy. Stick to your list to avoid impulse purchases.

  o **Use coupons and discounts:** Look for coupons and discounts online or in-store to save money on purchases.

  o **Buy in bulk:** Consider buying in bulk for items you use frequently, such as toilet paper or laundry detergent. This can help you save money over time.

  o **Compare prices:** Before making a purchase, compare prices online or at different stores to find the best deal.

  o **Avoid debt:** Try to avoid using credit cards or taking out loans unless absolutely necessary. This can help you avoid unnecessary interest charges and fees.

  o **Increase your income:** Look for ways to increase your income, such as taking on extra work or starting a side hustle. The more you earn, the more you can save.

o **Automate savings:** Set up automatic transfers from your checking account into a savings account or investment account. This can help you save without having to think about it.

o **Track your spending:** Keep track of your expenses and review your budget regularly to identify areas where you can cut back.

o **Set financial goals:** Set specific financial goals, such as saving for a down payment on a house or paying off debt, and work towards them. Having a goal in mind can help you stay motivated and focused on saving.

+ **Shop around for better deals:** Compare prices for services like insurance, utilities, and phone plans to find the best deals.

+ **Automate savings:** Set up automatic transfers from your checking account to your savings account or investment account to save consistently without thinking about it.

+ **Increase your income:** Look for ways to increase your income, such as taking on a side gig or asking for a raise at your job.

increasing your income can be a great way to optimize your spending and increase your savings rate. Here are some strategies you can use:

o **Negotiate a raise:** If you're employed, consider asking for a raise at your current job. Do some research to find out what the market rate is for your position and use that as leverage.

o **Take on a side hustle:** Consider taking on a side gig to earn extra income. You can use the extra money to pay off debt or increase your savings.

o **Rent out a spare room:** If you have a spare room in your home, consider renting it out on Airbnb or to a long-term tenant. This can be a good source of extra income.

o **Sell items you no longer need:** Take a look around your home and see if there are any items you no longer need that you can sell for extra cash.

o **Freelance or consult:** If you have a particular skill or expertise, consider freelancing or consulting in your spare time to earn extra income.

Remember, every little bit helps when it comes to increasing your savings rate.

+ **Avoid lifestyle inflation:** As your income increases, avoid increasing your expenses at the same rate. Instead, save or invest the extra money to build wealth over time.

+ **Use cash-back and rewards programs:** Use credit cards or apps that offer cash-back or rewards for purchases to earn money while you spend.

However, it's important to use these programs responsibly and pay off your balance in full each month to avoid interest charges and fees. Otherwise, any rewards earned may be outweighed by the cost of interest. It's also important to only use rewards programs for purchases you would make anyway, rather than spending extra just to earn rewards.

+ **Prioritize savings:** Make savings a priority in your budget and aim to save at least 20% of your income each month.

By optimizing your spending and increasing your savings rate, you can build wealth over time and achieve your financial goals more quickly.

Chapter 3: Building Your Financial Foundation

Building a strong financial foundation starts with preparing for the unexpected. That's where emergency funds and insurance come in.

An emergency fund is a savings account specifically set aside to cover unexpected expenses or emergencies, such as medical bills, car repairs, or job loss. The general rule of thumb is to have three to six months' worth of living expenses saved in your emergency fund.

Insurance is also an important part of financial security. It provides protection against unexpected events that could otherwise be financially devastating, such as illness, accidents, or property damage. Types of insurance you may need include health insurance, auto insurance, home or renter's insurance, and life insurance.

Having both an emergency fund and appropriate insurance coverage can provide peace of mind and help protect your finances in case of unforeseen events.

Setting financial goals and creating a plan to achieve them

Setting financial goals and creating a plan to achieve them is crucial to building a strong financial foundation. Without a plan, it can be difficult to know where to start and how to make progress towards your goals. Here are some steps you can take to set financial goals and create a plan to achieve them:

+ **Define your financial goals:** Start by defining your financial goals, both short-term and long-term. Short-term goals may include things like paying off credit card debt, while long-term goals may include saving for retirement or buying a home.

+ **Prioritize your goals:** Once you have identified your goals, prioritize them based on importance and urgency. This will help you focus your efforts on the goals that matter most.

+ **Set specific, measurable goals:** Make your goals specific and measurable so that you can track your progress and stay motivated. For example, instead of simply saying you want to save money, set a specific savings goal such as saving $10,000 for a down payment on a home within the next two years.

+ **Create an action plan:** Once you have defined your goals, create an action plan outlining the steps you need to take to achieve them. This may include creating a budget, paying off debt, or increasing your savings rate.

+ **Monitor your progress:** Regularly monitor your progress towards your goals and adjust your plan as needed.

Celebrate your successes and stay motivated by tracking your progress and seeing the results of your hard work.

Remember, setting financial goals and creating a plan to achieve them takes time and effort, but the rewards are worth it. By taking control of your finances and working towards your goals, you can build a strong financial foundation and achieve financial security.

Understanding the basics of investing and asset allocation

Investing is the act of putting money into an asset with the expectation of generating a return or profit. When it comes to investing, it's important to understand the concept of asset allocation. Asset allocation is the process of spreading your investments across different asset classes, such as stocks, bonds, and real estate, based on your investment goals, risk tolerance, and time horizon.

The main asset classes are stocks, bonds, and cash. Stocks are ownership shares of a company and represent a stake in the company's assets and profits. Bonds, on the other hand, are debt securities issued by governments or corporations. When you buy a bond, you are lending money to the issuer in exchange for a fixed income stream. Cash, or cash equivalents, are investments that can be easily converted to cash, such as money market funds or short-term government bonds.

When it comes to asset allocation, the mix of stocks, bonds, and cash that you choose will depend on several factors, including your investment goals, time horizon, risk tolerance, and current market conditions. Generally speaking, stocks tend to offer the highest potential for long-term returns but come with higher risks, while bonds tend to offer lower returns but come with lower risks. Cash investments, such as savings accounts or money market funds, offer very low returns but are very low risk.

It's important to note that asset allocation is not a one-time decision. As you get older and your investment goals and risk tolerance change, you may need to adjust your asset allocation to reflect these changes. Regularly rebalancing your portfolio to ensure that it remains aligned with your goals and risk tolerance is an important part of successful investing.

How to build a diversified investment portfolio

Building a diversified investment portfolio is crucial for managing risk and maximizing returns. Here are some tips to help you build a diversified portfolio:

- **Determine your risk tolerance:** Your risk tolerance will dictate how much risk you can handle in your portfolio. A higher risk tolerance may allow you to invest in riskier assets such as stocks, while a lower risk tolerance may lead you to invest in more conservative assets like bonds.

- **Spread your investments across asset classes:** To diversify your portfolio, invest in a variety of assets, such as stocks, bonds, and real estate. Different asset classes have different risk and return characteristics, so spreading your investments across them can help mitigate risk.

- **Invest in different sectors:** Within each asset class, invest in different sectors. For example, in the stock market, invest in sectors such as technology, healthcare, and finance, rather than just one sector.

- **Invest in different geographic regions:** Investing in different geographic regions can also help diversify your portfolio. Consider investing in international stocks and bonds in addition to domestic ones.

- **Rebalance your portfolio regularly:** Over time, your portfolio may become unbalanced due to changes in the market. Rebalancing your portfolio periodically can help ensure that your investments remain diversified and aligned with your investment goals and risk tolerance.

- **Consider using index funds or ETFs:** Index funds and ETFs can provide diversification across multiple stocks or bonds, making them an efficient and cost-effective way to build a diversified portfolio.

Remember, diversification does not guarantee against loss, but it can help mitigate risk and improve your chances of achieving your investment goals.

Chapter 4: Accelerating Your Financial Progress

Strategies for increasing your income and earning potential

Here are some strategies for increasing your income and earning potential:

⁜ Develop new skills

Take courses or classes to learn new skills that are in demand in your industry or that can help you transition to a higher-paying job.

that's a great strategy for increasing your income and earning potential. Learning new skills can help you qualify for higher-paying jobs or increase your value to your current employer, leading to opportunities for raises or promotions. Some options for developing new skills include taking courses at a local college or university, attending workshops or conferences, or pursuing online learning opportunities. It's important to identify which skills are in demand in your industry and focus on building those skills to maximize your earning potential.

⁜ Negotiate your salary

If you're already employed, ask for a raise or negotiate a higher starting salary when accepting a new job offer.

Here are some tips to help you negotiate:

- o **Do your research:** Research the average salary range for your position and industry in your location. This information can help you determine a fair salary to negotiate for.

- o **Highlight your accomplishments:** Prepare a list of your accomplishments and contributions to the company. Show how you have added value and how you have exceeded expectations.

- o **Practice your pitch:** Practice your negotiation pitch and be confident in your skills and accomplishments.

- o **Be willing to compromise:** If your employer is not able to meet your salary expectations, be willing to negotiate other benefits such as additional vacation time or a flexible work schedule.

Remember that negotiating your salary is a normal part of the hiring process and can help you earn what you are worth.

- **Freelance or start a side hustle:** Consider working on a freelance or contract basis, or starting a side business or gig to generate additional income.

- **Invest in yourself:** Invest in your education, certifications, or personal development to increase your knowledge and expertise and make yourself more valuable in your industry.

Here are some ways to do it:

- o **Education:** Consider going back to school to earn a degree or taking courses to improve your skills and knowledge. This can make you more qualified for higher-paying jobs.

- o **Certifications:** Obtaining certifications in your field can increase your credibility and make you more competitive in the job market.

- o **Networking:** Attend networking events, join professional organizations, and connect with industry leaders to gain insights, learn about job opportunities, and develop important relationships.

- o **Personal development:** Develop soft skills such as communication, leadership, and time management, which can make you more effective and valuable in your job.

o **Health and wellness:** Prioritizing your physical and mental health can help you be more productive and focused at work, potentially leading to better job performance and higher earnings.

+ **Look for new opportunities:** Keep an eye out for job openings or promotions within your company, or explore job opportunities in other industries or companies that offer higher salaries or better benefits.

Here are some more strategies for increasing your income and earning potential:

o **Maximize your current income:** If you're not able to increase your income through a raise or promotion, look for ways to maximize the income you already have. This might include asking for overtime, taking on additional responsibilities, or finding ways to increase your productivity and efficiency.

o **Sell unused items:** Sell unused items in your home or garage to earn some extra cash. This could include clothing, electronics, furniture, or other items that are in good condition but no longer serve a purpose for you.

o **Rent out your property:** If you have extra space in your home or a vacation property, consider renting it out on a short-term or long-term basis to generate additional income.

o **Invest in dividend-paying stocks:** Consider investing in stocks that pay dividends, which can provide a regular source of passive income.

o **Take advantage of tax benefits:** Maximize your tax savings by taking advantage of tax-deferred retirement accounts, such as a 401(k) or IRA, and deductions for business expenses if you have a side hustle.

- **Network:** Build relationships with colleagues, mentors, and industry leaders to gain insights and access to new opportunities. Attend industry events and join professional organizations to expand your network.

- **Leverage technology:** Take advantage of online platforms and tools to monetize your skills, such as creating online courses or selling digital products.

Here are some ways you can use technology to monetize your skills:

o **Create an online course:** If you have expertise in a particular area, you can create an online course and sell it on platforms like Udemy, Teachable, or Skillshare.

o **Sell digital products:** If you're a graphic designer or artist, you can sell your designs or artwork on platforms like Etsy, Creative Market, or Society6.

o **Become a freelancer:** You can use platforms like Upwork, Fiverr, or Freelancer to find freelance work and offer your services to clients around the world.

o **Offer coaching or consulting services:** If you have expertise in a particular field, you can offer coaching or consulting services online using tools like Zoom or Skype.

o **Start a blog or podcast:** If you enjoy writing or talking about a particular topic, you can start a blog or podcast and monetize it through advertising, sponsorships, or affiliate marketing.

o **Sell physical products online:** You can use platforms like Amazon or Shopify to sell physical products online, such as handmade crafts, clothing, or home decor.

o **Participate in online surveys or focus groups:** While

this may not generate a significant income, participating in online surveys or focus groups can be a quick and easy way to earn some extra cash.

Remember, increasing your income takes time and effort, but the benefits of doing so can have a significant impact on your financial progress.

Tips for creating multiple streams of income

Creating multiple streams of income can help increase your financial stability and security. Here are some tips for creating multiple streams of income:

+ **Diversify your income sources:** Instead of relying solely on your day job, explore other sources of income such as rental properties, stocks, or starting a side business.

+ **Leverage your skills:** Consider using your skills and expertise to offer consulting services or freelance work on platforms like Upwork or Fiverr.

   Leveraging your skills can be a great way to create multiple streams of income. In addition to consulting and freelance work, you can also consider teaching online courses, creating digital products, or offering coaching services. The key is to find ways to monetize your skills and expertise in different ways.

+ **Monetize your hobbies:** If you have a hobby or passion, explore ways to monetize it. For example, if you love photography, consider selling your photos online or offering photography services.

+ **Invest in real estate:** Real estate can provide a steady stream of passive income through rental income or property appreciation.

+ **Build a passive income stream:** Look for opportunities to earn passive income, such as investing in dividend-paying stocks or creating digital products like ebooks or online courses.

- **Start a side hustle:** Consider starting a side hustle, such as selling handmade products on Etsy or driving for a ride-sharing service like Uber or Lyft.

- **Take advantage of the gig economy:** The gig economy offers a variety of opportunities to earn extra income, such as delivering groceries or food, pet-sitting, or completing tasks on TaskRabbit.

How to leverage your skills and expertise to increase your earnings

you can consider the following tips:

- **Identify your unique skills:** Identify your unique skills and strengths that you can use to create value for others. These can be skills from your professional or personal experience.

- **Choose a target market:** Once you have identified your skills, choose a target market that would be interested in your skills. This could be a specific industry or group of people.

- **Create a product or service:** Develop a product or service that solves a problem for your target market. For example, if you're a graphic designer, you could offer custom branding services for small businesses.

- **Market yourself:** Use social media and other marketing channels to promote your product or service. You can also network with potential clients and partners to get the word out about your offerings.

- **Provide exceptional value:** Provide exceptional value to your clients by delivering high-quality work and excellent customer service. This will help you build a positive reputation and attract repeat business and referrals.

- **Continuously improve:** Continuously improve your skills and offerings to stay ahead of the competition and offer the best possible service to your clients.

By leveraging your skills and expertise, you can create additional income streams and increase your earning potential.

The power of passive income and how to create it

Passive income refers to the money you earn without being actively involved in the earning process. This type of income is often generated from investments, rental properties, or businesses that you own but don't manage actively. Passive income has the potential to provide financial freedom and can be a valuable source of income, especially when you are retired or looking to supplement your primary income.

Here are some ways to create passive income:

- o **Investing in stocks:** Investing in stocks that pay dividends can provide a regular source of passive income. Dividends are a portion of a company's earnings that are paid out to shareholders.

- o **Real estate investing:** Real estate can provide a steady stream of passive income through rental income or property appreciation.

- o **Creating digital products:** Creating digital products like ebooks, online courses, or software can provide a source of passive income once the product is created.

- o **Peer-to-peer lending:** Peer-to-peer lending platforms like LendingClub or Prosper allow you to lend money to borrowers and earn interest on your investment.

- o **Affiliate marketing:** Affiliate marketing involves promoting products and services and earning a commission for each sale made through your referral link.

- o **Renting out assets:** Renting out assets like a spare room on Airbnb or a car on Turo can provide passive income.

o **Royalties:** If you are a writer, musician, or artist, you can earn royalties from your work through platforms like Amazon KDP or Spotify.

It's important to note that creating passive income requires an initial investment of time, effort, and often money. However, once established, passive income streams can provide a source of income for years to come.

Chapter 5: Staying Motivated and on Track

Staying motivated is crucial to achieving financial success. It can be easy to get discouraged or distracted along the way, especially when facing setbacks or challenges. However, by staying focused and motivated, you can overcome obstacles and achieve your financial goals.

There are several ways to stay motivated on your financial journey, including:

- o **Visualize your goals:** Take some time to visualize what your life will be like when you achieve your financial goals. Create a vision board or write down your goals and the benefits of achieving them. This will help you stay motivated and focused on your goals.

- o **Celebrate small wins:** Celebrate each milestone you achieve along the way, no matter how small. This will help you stay motivated and build momentum toward your larger goals.

- o **Find an accountability partner:** Partner with someone who can hold you accountable and provide support along the way. This can be a friend, family member, or financial advisor.

- o **Stay informed:** Stay up-to-date on financial news and trends to stay motivated and informed about your financial decisions.

- o **Track your progress:** Keep track of your progress toward your financial goals. This will help you see how far you've come and stay motivated to keep going.

- o **Reward yourself:** When you reach a major financial milestone or achieve a significant goal, reward yourself. This will help you stay motivated and encourage you to keep working toward your next goal.

Overall, staying motivated is key to achieving financial success. By visualizing your goals, celebrating small wins, finding an accountability partner, staying informed, tracking your progress, and rewarding yourself, you can stay motivated and on track toward your financial goals.

How to overcome obstacles and stay focused on your goals

Here are some tips for overcoming obstacles and staying focused on your financial goals:

- o **Identify and address limiting beliefs:** Sometimes our own beliefs and mindset can hold us back from achieving our goals. Identify any limiting beliefs you have about money or your ability to achieve financial success and work on shifting them to more positive, empowering beliefs.

- o **Break down your goals:** Large goals can feel overwhelming and unattainable, making it easy to lose motivation. Break down your goals into smaller, more manageable steps that you can work on consistently over time. This will help you build momentum and stay motivated.

- o **Track your progress:** Keep track of your progress towards your goals. This will help you see the progress you've made and provide motivation to continue. Celebrate your milestones along the way to stay encouraged.

- o **Stay accountable:** Share your goals with someone you trust, such as a friend, family member, or mentor, and ask them to hold you accountable. You can also consider joining a support group or finding an accountability partner to help you stay on track.

- o **Learn from setbacks:** Setbacks and failures are a natural part of any journey. Instead of getting discouraged, use setbacks as an opportunity to learn and grow. Identify what went wrong and use that knowledge to adjust your approach and move forward.

- ○ **Focus on the why:** Remind yourself of why you set your financial goals in the first place. This will help you stay motivated and focused, even when faced with challenges or obstacles.

Tools and resources for tracking your progress and staying accountable

There are several tools and resources that can help you track your progress and stay accountable on your financial journey:

- **Budgeting apps:** Budgeting apps like Mint, YNAB, and Personal Capital can help you track your spending, monitor your savings, and set financial goals.

- **Investment tracking tools:** Investment tracking tools like SigFig and Personal Capital can help you track your investments and monitor your portfolio performance.

- **Debt repayment calculators:** If you're working on paying off debt, debt repayment calculators like Undebt.it and Bankrate's debt repayment calculator can help you create a plan and track your progress.

- **Financial advisors:** A financial advisor can provide personalized advice and guidance to help you reach your financial goals.

- **Support groups:** Joining a support group or finding an accountability partner can provide the motivation and encouragement you need to stay on track.

- **Personal development resources:** Personal development resources, such as books, podcasts, and online courses, can help you develop the mindset and habits needed to achieve financial success.

Strategies for celebrating your successes and staying motivated for the long term

Celebrating your successes is an important part of staying motivated on your financial journey. Here are some strategies to help you celebrate your successes and stay motivated for the long term:

- o **Set small milestones:** Break down your long-term financial goals into smaller milestones. Celebrate each milestone as you achieve it. This will help you stay motivated and keep you focused on your progress.

- o **Reward yourself:** When you reach a milestone or achieve a financial goal, reward yourself. This could be something small like treating yourself to a nice meal or buying something you've been wanting for a while.

- o **Share your successes:** Share your successes with family and friends. Celebrating with others will make your accomplishments feel more real and give you a sense of pride and accomplishment.

- o **Keep track of your progress:** Use a financial tracker to monitor your progress. Seeing how far you've come can be a great motivator to keep going.

- o **Stay positive:** Staying positive and maintaining a positive outlook can help you stay motivated. Focus on your progress and the things you've achieved rather than any setbacks you may have experienced.

- o **Take breaks:** Taking a break from your financial journey can help you stay motivated over the long term. Take time to relax and recharge so you can come back to your financial goals with renewed energy and focus.

Conclusion

Recap of key takeaways from the book

Key Takeaways from the book are:

1. **The importance of taking control of your finances and understanding your personal financial situation.**

2. **The benefits of setting financial goals and creating a plan to achieve them.**

3. **The importance of budgeting and living within your means.**

4. **The value of saving and investing for the future.**

5. **Strategies for increasing your income and building multiple streams of income.**

6. **The power of passive income and how to create it.**

7. **The importance of staying motivated and on track with your financial goals.**

By implementing these key takeaways, you can create a solid financial foundation, achieve your financial goals, and create a more secure and stable future for yourself and your family. Remember that financial success is a journey, not a destination, and staying motivated and focused on your goals is key to long-term success.

Final words of advice for achieving financial success

achieving financial success requires a combination of knowledge, discipline, and perseverance. By creating a strong financial foundation, setting clear goals, and taking consistent action towards those goals, you can achieve financial security and freedom. It's important to stay motivated, overcome obstacles, and hold yourself accountable to ensure you stay on track. Remember that financial success is a journey, and it's important to celebrate your successes along the way. With the right mindset and strategies, anyone can achieve financial success and live the life they desire.

How to continue learning and growing on your financial journey.

Continuing to learn and grow on your financial journey is crucial to achieving long-term success. Here are some ways to continue your education and stay up to date on the latest financial trends and strategies:

1. **Read financial books and articles: There are countless books and articles available on personal finance and investing. Continuously seek out new resources to broaden your knowledge and gain new insights.**

2. **Attend financial workshops and seminars: Many financial institutions and organizations offer workshops and seminars on topics such as investing, retirement planning, and budgeting. Attending these events can provide valuable information and networking opportunities.**

3. **Join online communities: There are numerous online communities focused on personal finance and investing. Joining these groups can provide a wealth of information, resources, and support.**

4. **Work with a financial advisor: If you're looking for personalized advice and guidance, consider working with a financial advisor. A good advisor can help you develop a comprehensive financial plan and provide ongoing support and education.**

5. **Remember, achieving financial success is a journey, not a destination. Stay focused on your goals, continue to learn and grow, and celebrate your successes along the way.**

ABOUT THE AUTHOR

Thank you for reading book.